Matt Talbot

An Introduction

GW00640771

MATT TALBOT

AN INTRODUCTION

VERITAS

Published 2017 by Veritas Publications
7–8 Lower Abbey Street
Dublin 1, Ireland
publications@veritas.ie
www.veritas.ie

ISBN 978 1 84730 799 6

10 9 8 7 6 5 4 3 2 1

The material included in this book is taken from *Remembering Matt Talbot* by Mary Purcell, first published by M.H. Gill and Sons Ltd, 1954; reprinted by Veritas Publications, 1990.

A catalogue record for this book is available from the British Library.

Designed by Heather Costello, Veritas Publications
Printed in the Republic of Ireland by SPRINT-print Ltd, Dublin

Veritas books are printed on paper made from the wood pulp of managed forests. For every tree felled, at least one tree is planted, thereby renewing natural resources.

Contents

Early Life

For Dubliners, Friday 2 May 1856 was a holiday. Law courts and public offices remained closed; the shops were shut. A grand parade was on its way from the Phoenix Park through the city centre to Dublin Castle to celebrate the end of the Crimean War.

At 13 Aldborough Court, Charles Talbot's wife was visited by neighbouring women who commiserated with her for having missed all the excitement. Elizabeth Talbot had more pressing concerns to keep her at home. On that day her second son, the boy she would call Matthew, was born.

Charles Talbot and Elizabeth Bagnall were married in the church of St John the Baptist, Clontarf, on 19 September 1853. Charles had a home for his wife, a room in a not too dilapidated tenement house, No. 2 Lower Rutland Street. His earnings were fifteen shillings a week and he was in fairly regular employment. Thirty years old at the time of his marriage, he was a very small man with a rather aggressive manner. Little did Elizabeth Talbot think when she settled down in Rutland Street in 1853 that within the next twenty years she would change her address no less than eleven times.

Between 1854 and 1874 Mrs Talbot gave birth to twelve children, nine of whom survived. Some were baptised in the Pro-Cathedral, some in St Agatha's Church, North William Street. The parents' addresses, recorded in the registers of these two churches, show their constant moving about from one drab lane or street to the next, from one crowded tenement house to another. Rutland Street, Summerhill, Aldborough Court, Newcomen Court, Montgomery Street, Byrne's Lane, Love Lane and other places long since demolished saw the Talbot family come and go. Their worst dwelling was in Love Lane, Ballybough; they spent most of the 1870s there before moving to a cottage in Newcomen Avenue off the North Strand.

In Matt Talbot's childhood there was no dole, no pensions, no children's allowances, no welfare clinics, no social services. Even water, that basic necessity, was not available in houses in slum areas. Citizens of Rutland Street and similar districts had to fetch every drop they needed from public fountains and horse troughs.

Dublin's population in 1850 was a quarter of a million. The city proper covered an area of about three thousand five hundred acres and was almost enclosed in the nine-mile-circuit formed by the North and South Circular

Roads. Two schools in the centre of that area claim the privilege of having had Matt Talbot on their rolls.

His first was St Laurence O'Toole's Christian Brothers' School; he was admitted on 8 July 1864. His older brother John had been a pupil in the same school from 1863; their address was given as Newcomen Court and their father's occupation as 'a cooper'.

Beyond a report on Matt stating that he was, 'kept at home through necessity', little is known of his progress, if any, in St Laurence O'Toole's. In May 1867 John and Matt were both admitted to O'Connell School, North Richmond Street, also run by the Christian Brothers. Matt was in a 'special' class, one for poor boys not likely to attend regularly or for a long period. They were taught the rudiments of reading and writing, learned their prayers, were given religious instruction and prepared for the sacraments.

Two men who remembered Matt in the Men's Sodality attached to St Francis Xavier church, the Jesuit church in Gardiner Street, said that he had a very pleasant singing voice, 'but a big voice for his size. You wouldn't know where a man so small got so powerful a voice'. Pat Doyle was in his nineties when interviewed in 1952; he knew all the Talbot boys, some of them being his close companions. He explained Matt's strong voice as inherited: 'He had a great shout, though he was such a bit of a man. And why wouldn't he? Sure the father had the very same shout; you'd hear oul' Charlie a mile away if one of the lads ruz his temper.'

Alas, Matt's academic record was not brilliant. Two words served as his report for 1867, his first year at O'Connell School: 'A Mitcher'. For 1868 the brief report ran: 'Kept at home through necessity', a comment that had also been made in one of his reports from St Laurence O'Toole's. That year the sum total of his attendance was three weeks, long enough to prepare for first Confession and Communion; in the following year he again spent three weeks in school and was prepared for Confirmation; but he considered himself a past pupil by then and was one of many boys who returned, unwillingly in most cases, to the evening religious class. His school career really ended in 1868 when he was twelve years old and eligible for work.

A twelve-year-old illiterate boy from Rutland Street was lucky to find work in the Dublin of 1868. Though business was brisk enough at the port, industry in Dublin and throughout Ireland had suffered a massive decline since the famine. One had to eat to live, and work that promised regular meals was most popular in a country still in the shadow of the Great Hunger.

Matt Talbot got employment as a messenger boy with the firm of E. and J. Burke at their stores in the North Lotts. The Burkes were wine merchants who also did bottling for Guinness' Brewery and for the Edinburgh brewers, Youngers. They had offices on the quays, at 16 Bachelors' Walk, and at 59 Abbey Street. He spent four years there and earned about four or five shillings a week, but in his next job he got six shillings a week, which was considered a fair wage for a boy messenger. The secretary employed by Burkes in 1953 remembered a very old employee who knew Matt Talbot from 1868 to 1872 'and could not say much to his credit concerning his time in our bottling stores'.

At Burkes', he found it easy to help himself to a pint of porter whenever he felt like it; there were evenings when he arrived home drunk. By the time he was sixteen his father, in charge of the bonded stores at the Custom House docks, got Matt a job as a messenger boy there. John, then eighteen, had not mitched from school and, having mastered the 'three Rs', was already moving up to a responsible position in the Port & Docks Board. The boys were the third generation of Talbots employed there, their grandfather Robert being on the payroll as well as their father. As for Matt, if, while at Burkes, he had come home drunk from a surfeit of Guinness, he now began to come home drunk on whiskey.

The Dark Years

By 1870 the Talbots had moved to 5 Love Lane, Ballybough, a worse tenement than any of their previous homes. One boy, Charles, had died in childhood. Between 1871 and 1874 Patrick, Susan and a second Charles were born. At the time of Charles' birth, John, Matt, Bob and probably Joe and Mary were working, but the family was poorer than ever, most of the earnings being spent on drink.

Tommy Ward, a family friend, remembered playing Hunt-the-Cap, a favourite game of small boys in the Dublin of his boyhood, with the younger Talbot lads. He stated that Matt's father was often drunk on Saturdays, 'and very quarrelsome, too, when he had drink in'. As for his brother Phil, who was seldom seen sober, 'He'd come rollin' up the North Strand, shouting, "I'm the Man, Talbot", and roarin' songs.'

In the 1860s over one thousand licensed premises and almost as many unlicensed shebeens were doing good business with Dublin's population of a quarter of a million. Arrests for drunkenness during 1865 numbered more than sixteen thousand, one-third of those arrested being women. Each year saw the number of deaths from intoxication rise; in 1862 there were four, by 1866 the number had risen to nineteen. Among the customs that spread throughout the city was an accepted system by which workmen were paid on Saturdays in the public house nearest their place of work. They were paid in cash or had their pay-cheques or pay-orders cashed by the publican. Naturally, the latter took it for granted that, in return for his financial services, the men would spend some of their earnings on his premises.

A niece of Matt Talbot heard her grandmother, Matt's mother, tell of how Matt would come home on Saturday evenings, hand his mother a shilling, all that remained of his wages, and say, 'Here, mother, is that any good to you?' And Mrs Talbot, a patient woman, would reply, 'God forgive you, Matt! Is that the way to treat your mother?' Once Matt and his brothers stole a fiddle from a street musician, sold it and bought drink with the proceeds. More than once he came home without even a shilling for his mother; he would patter in barefoot, having pawned his boots to pay for his addiction. He attended Mass but during the early 1880s showed no further interest in religion. His family — aggressive, rowdy and quarrelsome — was not, except for the mother, the girls and John, a very exemplary one; their home was no haven of peace.

Matt left the Port & Docks Stores in 1882 when his father retired and worked as a hodman for Pemberton's, the building contractors; he remained with that firm for some years, gaining the reputation of being a good worker. Although a man of small build, the drive and pugnacity of the Talbot blood spurred him on to prove that he was as good a worker as the biggest and brawniest man on the job. As Pat Doyle related, foremen got wise to this and put him first on the line of hodmen 'to set the pace'. He seems to have worked for alternate periods at Pembertons and at the Port & Docks, but whenever he was back with the latter firm it was as a docker, not at the Bonded Stores. Some supervisor must have noted that Charles and Matt Talbot were very partial to 'spirituous liquors'. John Talbot, however, was kept on and was promoted.

On one of the few occasions in later life when Matt referred to his earlier days he said: 'I should be the last person to advise anyone about religion. When I was young I was very careless about religion because of drink; and I broke my mother's heart'.

The Road to Redemption

A never-to-be-forgotten day in Matt Talbot's life took place in the summer of 1884. For an entire week he stayed away from work and spent the time drinking heavily. By Saturday he was penniless, as was his brother Joe. Being 'on the slate' in local public houses they could not hope for further credit. They stood near O'Meara's pub on the North Strand, a strategic position on that day and at that hour. Dockers would be knocking off work for the weekly half-day and would come to the pub to draw, and drink, their pay. Among them would be friends whom the Talbots had often treated and Matt and Joe expected that the compliment would be returned now.

They were disappointed. For some reason not one man asked them 'if they had a mouth on them' – perhaps the two brothers had cadged drinks too often. Joe stayed on, still hoping. Matt turned on his heel and walked home. His mother, surprised to see him home so early and quite sober, was more surprised when he looked for a clean shirt, tidied himself up and announced that he was going to Holy Cross College, a diocesan seminary, to take the pledge. Mrs Talbot was not impressed; she did not think Matt capable of keeping a pledge. 'Go, in God's name,' she said, 'but don't take it unless you are going to keep it'.

On the following morning, Sunday, he received Holy Communion at Mass. More surprises awaited his mother. On Monday, Matt rose very early and went to five o'clock Mass in Gardiner Street church before going on to work at six. He had no trouble finding work as his reputation for being a good worker was well-known. Builders and the Port & Docks Board had him regularly on their pay-rolls; he also worked as a temporary hand in T. & C. Martin's timber-yards.

Very little is known of Matt Talbot during the decade between 1884 and 1894. His mother told how he was sorely tempted to break his pledge, but when the three months were up he went back to Holy Cross and renewed it for six months and then renounced drink for life. He continued to go to early Mass daily and in the evenings, to avoid his former drinking companions, he went to a church and remained there praying until the church closed. Soon he was a familiar figure in Gardiner Street, Phibsboro and Berkeley Road churches.

Hardly anyone, not even his mother, realised what a complete conversion Matt's had been. Beyond the fact that he kept the pledge, repaid his debts, steered clear of his former 'drinking butties' and prayed constantly, his life, to all appearances, showed little trace of the tremendous interior renewal that had begun in 1884 and was steadily progressing.

He was the same Matt Talbot, the same unskilled labourer, the same unimportant citizen of contemporary Dublin. In one sense at least he had found permanent employment. To the service of God he brought the same verve and determination, the natural tenacity that had always distinguished him. Summing up his character, Pat Doyle said, 'Matt could never go easy, at anything'. The reserves of energy, the indomitable will that had hitherto dragged him down, now spurred him in a different direction.

His calling in life was a humble one, to fetch and carry for the trained men who specialised in certain trades and crafts. His daily work involved the carrying of bricks, mortar, heavy and hard-to-balance planks. A man bearing such loads walks with his head bowed, his eyes continually on the ground; he is careful when mounting ladders, he takes the measure of passages through which he must manoeuvre unwieldy loads. Not for him to stand with foreman or architect, admiring this facade, watching that beam being swung into position. From the little we know of Matt Talbot during the first decade of his changed life there emerges a man intent on humbling and hiding himself, a worker attentive to his tasks, diligent and constant in all his occupations, spiritual and temporal.

Matt did not adopt the austerities associated with his name in the years immediately following his conversion. His friend John Robins told how Matt, to keep his mind off drink in the years after 1884, became a heavy smoker, smoking up to seven ounces of tobacco some weeks. 'When he decided to give that up he went to his confessor and took a pledge against it.' Paddy Laird recalled how his father, Bob, would bring Matt to their home when Paddy was a young lad and Matt would accept a cup of tea and whatever Mrs Laird offered with it.

Mrs Andrews and Mrs Fylan, sisters of Matt, giving evidence in 1937, twelve years after their brother's death, stated under oath:

> After work until about ten o'clock Matt was hardly ever off his knees; he even ate his dinner on his knees. If someone called to visit he would sit down. At that time (1884-1894) he might take meat once

or twice a week, or eggs for dinner. During Lent he took nothing only dry bread and cocoa, shell cocoa. Sometimes, but never on a Wednesday or a Friday, a little fish. He fasted from meat all June in honour of the Sacred Heart and the same for a week before big feastdays and the same in Advent ... He often referred to his past sins, saying, 'Where would I be only for God and his Blessed Mother?' He had a little statue of Our Lady and used to say, 'No one knows the good mother she has been to me.'

Still, Matt was occasionally tempted to return to his old ways. One evening he stood near a pub in Dorset Street, fingering the coins in his pocket, remembering the taste of porter, of whiskey. Finally he went in. None of the customers were men he knew and, though he waited a long time, no barman came to serve him; so he left, went to Gardiner Street church nearby and remained there praying until the church closed for the night. After that incident he never carried money on him again until late in life when he brought it to people in need or for charity collections.

When Fr Cullen, a Jesuit, founded the Pioneer Association, Matt Talbot was one of the first to join. It is interesting to note that when he sought compensation in smoking for his self-imposed sobriety, thus turning from one addiction to another, he got his confessor to administer a pledge against tobacco to him.

Although we do not know who his regular confessor was from 1884 to 1896 we do know that early in that period Matt learned to read. For an illiterate man in his thirties it must have been a herculean task. Possibly his brother John, 'the only steady one of the Talbots and a great scholar,' according to Pat Doyle, helped him.

His heart must have failed him often in his struggles with the printed word and memories of days spent mitching from Brother Ryan's 'special class' for backward boys must have risen to reproach him. His experience in taking the pledge had helped; strength to stand firm was there for the asking as he found by praying when tempted to start drinking again. Similarly, when he encountered difficulties in reading he prayed for help, to the Holy Spirit, to Our Lady and the angels and saints.

First among the books he read at this and at all later periods of his life were the Scriptures. Because he was still only learning to read he went very slowly, so all that he read got time to sink in. He had several copies of the

Bible, besides copies of the New Testament and a separate copy of St John's Gospel. He marked the fiftieth psalm, the Miserere, he had leaflets with this psalm, and he also marked two other penitential psalms and two chapters from the Book of Wisdom, Solomon's Prayer for Wisdom being on a well-thumbed page.

A Man of Zeal

The road Matt Talbot set out to travel in 1884 was a long and hard one, a road that was to stretch more than forty years into the future. He was the same Matt and had to accept himself as he was, with the same lingering wish for drink, the same Talbot temper with its short fuse; but he had, too, the same ability to work, to persevere with a task until it was finished.

Conversion, even the most dramatic, has its stages. In Matt's case, apart from turning away from drink and whatever sinfulness he acknowledged when he made a sincere confession the day he took his first pledge, there was a slow but steady progress towards holiness. At a time when most men went to confession once or twice a year, he went weekly and to priests who were wise and experienced directors. They were men who advised him well, helped him to see and correct whatever stood between him and God, restraining him in the early years, encouraging him later to follow the inspirations received when the Lord invited him to 'Go up higher, friend' on the paths of prayer and penance.

While waiting for the church doors to be opened before five o'clock Mass in Gardiner Street, Matt would kneel on the steps, praying, if no one was around; but if others had gathered he would wait on the steps of the convent nearby, fearing that the conversation of those at the church door would impede his concentration on his prayer. On entering the church he would kneel and kiss the floor, then go to Our Lady's altar and light a candle before proceeding to his usual place, a pew from which he could see three altars. In those pre-Vatican II days, Masses were offered simultaneously at different altars.

Apart altogether from the spiritual content of the books Matt read at the turn of the century, it is noticeable that he became increasingly capable of reading and appreciating books that made considerable demands on his memory and intelligence, books on controversial issues that required him to reason and arrive at conclusions.

For one thing, after 1895 Matt's reading covered a wider range. Apart from commentaries on the Scriptures, books on prayer and the spiritual life and lives of the saints there were also historical works, doctrinal treatises and booklets and pamphlets on controversial subjects. By this time Matt seems to have overcome his early difficulties in reading and was intent on accumulating stores of secular as well as spiritual knowledge.

In 1899 Matt's father died, and Matt and his mother left Middle Gardiner Street for 18 Upper Rutland Street where Matt rented the basement. It was at this time that he added further penances to the severe fasting that had been his practice for more than a decade. His sister, Mrs Fylan, told how he slept:

> He slept on a broad plank the width of the bed, and he had a wooden block for a pillow. These he kept covered with a sheet and light blanket ... When I saw the plank and block first they were lying against the wall. When I asked him what they were for, all he said was, 'they're for a purpose'.

Again, some instinct drew him to imitate the austere streak that distinguished ancient Irish piety. Matt Talbot's penitential practices scandalise some in an age when bodily ease and comfort have prior importance. Each day during Lent and again in June he observed a complete 'black fast', i.e. using no milk and taking only two light meals without meat or butter. Outside of these times his usual diet was meagre. On Sundays his first meal of the day, after hearing several Masses, was at two o'clock; if it was fairly substantial, he ate nothing else that day; if that meal was light he allowed himself cocoa or tea and bread in the evening. On the days he took meat he often asked his sister to cook fish instead; then he would tell her to take the fish home with her and leave the water she used to boil it; he would then dunk his dry bread in the fishy liquid. His sister used to say:

> I don't know how our Matt exists on the small amount of food he eats. Yet, in spite of his fasting he always looked well and healthy and was not emaciated looking. And he was well able to do his work, which was hard work.

When, in his late sixties Matt's health broke down and he had to stay away from work and attend hospital, he ate whatever the doctor ordered, and when in hospital, or in a friend's house, would eat whatever was placed before him. He curtailed sleep to a minimum, usually allowing himself four hours sleep each night and that on a comfortless bed.

Mrs Talbot told her daughters that often she woke at night to find Matt praying, with arms out-stretched, until four in the morning but she warned them not to speak of this to anyone outside the family.

Later in his life, when other workmen asked Matt Talbot why he had never married, he replied that it would have interfered with the manner of life he intended to live. His mother told his sisters that he had once considered the matter but decided against marrying. Mrs Talbot was the only person taken into his confidence at the time. He was on building work at the home of a leading Protestant clergyman. The cook there, noticing that he did not flirt or joke with the maids like his workmates, spoke to him one day. She informed him that she had saved sufficient money to buy and furnish a house and ended by proposing marriage.

Matt said that he would consider her proposal and pray about it. After making a Novena he told the girl, a Catholic, that he had been enlightened and had come to the conclusion that he had better remain single. There is no clue to the cook's identity or to her reaction. Once, when a friend asked him why he had not married, he said that the Blessed Virgin told him not to.

Though Matt was by this time proficient in reading, his handwriting was poor, likewise his spelling. He had table-books and ready reckoners and other aids in his room and in his hut in T. & C. Martin's yard to help him make up bills.

At one time he was in the creosote boilers, where timber was dipped into the boiling tar, very hard work. Later he carried deal timber from the piles to the sawmills; later again he helped in the hardwood drying shed and after that he was in the part of the yard known as Castle Forbes. He was a good worker and very punctual; he wouldn't waste a minute. When waiting for a load of timber to arrive he'd avail of that time to pray or read; he always had pamphlets, lives of saints and the like, in his coat pocket.

Joe Nolan commented on Matt's build, which did not help to lessen the hard work he did:

> He was small and it often struck me that carrying the deals either to the stacks or to be creosoted must have been very hard on Matt, for he had the most sloping shoulders of any man I ever saw. You would wonder how he kept the planks from slipping off his shoulder with such a slope.

Mr O'Connor, the cashier, recalled how Matt made a practice of attending charity sermons preached throughout the city and suburbs. He would walk long distances to the churches where they were preached and would withdraw a pound note from the money Mr O'Connor held for him to pay into the collection for which the sermon was preached.

John Monaghan, clerk in Gardiner Street church, who often met Matt there, said, 'He would speak if you greeted him, but you had the impression that he would rather no one spoke to him. Matt wanted only the one thing: God.'

Matt on Strike

In 1913 Jim Larkin organised a strike against William Martin Murphy's Dublin Tramways Company. Murphy owned the *Irish Independent* newspaper. The timing was good, as it was Horse Show Week and Dublin was crowded with titled and wealthy people from Ireland and Britain when the tramway men simply stepped off their trams and left them on the street. Murphy immediately declared that in future he would not employ any unionised tramway men. Other employers followed his lead and there were 'lockouts' all over the city. Larkin retaliated by initiating 'sympathetic strike tactics'; this resulted in workers not previously involved coming out. Martin's men went on strike early in September, Matt Talbot with the rest.

It has been stated more than once, and publicly, that Matt Talbot was a strike-breaker who took no interest in his fellow workers' struggle for better conditions. This is quite untrue. Apart from the statements of men in Martin's, documents still preserved by his union utterly disprove this allegation. Matt joined the Builders-Labourers' Branch on 22 September 1911 and was a fully paid-up member when the 1913 strike began. He paid the strike levy. He did not carry a picket but neither did he pass one; men in his age-bracket, like Bob Laird, were not asked to picket. If he had 'scabbed' would not the union have expelled him? Yet, his name remained on the books and his branch paid him national health insurance benefit during his illness of 1923–24. At a workers' meeting held during the 1920s a visiting speaker called Matt 'a strike-breaker and a scab'; he was immediately shouted down and forced to withdraw the epithet.

A lot has been made of Matt's non-attendance at union meetings, especially during the strike; but he never read newspapers or public notices, never raised his eyes when walking along a street except when passing a church; the strike gave him the opportunity – which he gladly availed of – to spend the entire day in the church, mostly in St Francis Xavier's, Gardiner Street. Even today, when the labour movement is highly and efficiently organised, well-educated and articulate members often fail to show up at ordinary or even special meetings.

Several workers and other acquaintances of Matt Talbot gave sworn evidence concerning his attitude towards workers and employers, towards Jim Larkin and his stand during the Great Strike. James Tallon said:

> The 1913 strike troubled me and I asked Matt what were the rights of it. He said that it had worried him, too, but he spoke to a priest in Gardiner Street who gave him a book to read. In it he read that no one had the right to starve the poor into submission. 'That was enough for me and settled my conscience,' he said.

Frank Larkin, no relation of Jim Larkin, said:

> Matt had a great regard for Larkin and for anyone who worked for the good of others. He felt that Larkin had been let down by the men after the strike and spoke of their ingratitude towards their leader.

Matt's brother Joe took an active part in the strike. After the grim winter of 1913/14 the English unions refused to send any further financial support to the Dublin strikers. These, faced with no alternative but starvation, had to return on the employers' terms; men who had been prominent during the strike were in many cases not taken back. Joe Talbot was among those refused re-employment.

Although Matt's activity during the strike was not very remarkable, it was nonetheless useful; out of this scanty strike pay he managed to give money to fellow worker who were harder hit and whose children were threatened by hunger. At no time – before, during or after – had he ever curried favour with the bosses. He told a friend he had spent the time of the strike praying and reading.

While city and country tried to recover from the effects of the strike, the First World War broke out. At last there was work in plenty for the unemployed and the recruiting offices were busy. The rights and wrongs of small nations were widely discussed. Up and down Dublin streets military bands played 'It's a Long Way to Tipperary' and 'Pack up Your Troubles in your old Kit-bag'. Men in Martin's yards saw their sons in khaki, waving farewell from the troopships steaming out by the North Wall. Matt Talbot, who had a nephew bound for the trenches, would have waved with his workmates as the boys sailed away, while on the quays a band played 'Come back to Erin'.

A World in Flux

Autumn had turned to winter and the German armies had overrun Belgium and begun their invasion of France when Matt's nephew who had enlisted in the British Army, came home on his first leave. He called to see his uncle and laughed when Matt said that he didn't like to see his visitor 'in that uniform', and added, 'I wasn't joking'.

Later that winter Matt's mother died. She was almost eighty and had been an invalid during her final years, but was well looked after by Matt and her daughters who called daily while Matt was at work. Other tenants in the house described her as a very quiet old woman who prayed a lot. After her death Matt asked the landlord, a Mr Kelly, to allow him to change to an attic at 'the top front' of the house. The change was easily made. A man intent on his journey to God travels light. His possessions consisted of a bed-frame, with wooden plank and pillow, a billy-can, his library and the box that housed it ('Talbot's Box'), a crucifix, a statue of Our Lady and a collection of small religious pictures. There was hardly a happier man in Dublin than Matt, 'a man of no property', alone in his attic room. He was poor indeed, but wealthy in true wisdom and never lonely, for in God he lived, moved and had his being. When a neighbour complained to him of her loneliness since the death of someone dear to her, Matt exclaimed, 'But how could anyone be lonely with Our Lord in the Blessed Sacrament?'

His prayer-books of 1914 and 1915 contained scraps of papers with headlines of disasters – Allied losses, German losses – showing that the war caused him some anguish. To him the numbers of fatalities were important in that they meant souls to be prayed for. Men for whom Christ died were being hurled into eternity, perhaps unprepared. Small nations, whose rights were much in the news at the outbreak of war, were forgotten as the conflict gathered momentum. However, in the conflagration that lit Europe, one small nation began to seek a way to right her ancient wrongs.

Although Matt would discuss politics during the First World War when he visited Bob Laird's house, he avoided the subject in the home of his sister, Mrs Andrews. He would say, when there, 'No politics, now; mind God and no politics.' That was because one of the boys was fighting in France at the time and he feared that a discussion on the rights or wrongs of the war might cause dissension. However, the 1916 Rising and its aftermath was a different story. He would discuss the happenings with Bob and Paddy Laird on their way home from work. Once he referred to the executions of the leaders and the wholesale arrests and deportations that followed, and remarked, 'Our lads will now be all driven into secret societies', a comment as shrewd as it was far-seeing.

In terms of his own life Matt Talbot translated Christ's words: 'If any man love me, let him deny himself, take up his cross and follow me.' Holiness is nothing if not diverse in its manifestations. All times, all nations, all creeds and classes have recognised it. Yet it is rare, so rare that when it is encountered, some wonder and admire while some are scandalised. Living with a spiritual intensity far deeper than that of his fellow man, Matt was always 'seeking the things that are above', so he freed himself from anything that entangled his spirit and held him back.

His first step in self-denial was the hardest – he had a desperate craving for drink in the three months of 1884 after he took his first pledge. Though he had a longer struggle to rid himself of the tobacco habit, he found a way of overcoming his longing to smoke. He carried a white pebble in his pocket and when friends filled their pipes and lit up, Matt popped the pebble into his mouth and sucked it while the others puffed away. His closest friends all remarked on this, a practice which Matt abandoned when smoking lost its lure for him.

On Wednesday 13 April at precisely 7.45 a.m. an explosion rocked the area adjoining Martin's yards. The IRA had blown up the London and North Western Railway Hotel at the North Wall where a force of a hundred Auxiliaries and Black and Tans were sleeping.

The moment the explosion occurred the British troops began combing the vicinity. They came out firing, some still in their pyjamas. One of the first arrested was Matt Talbot, caught opening up Martin's yard. He was brought, with hands up, from his hut in Castle Forbes to the entrance gate, placed against a wall and searched; he was then released. Later that morning when he met Mrs Manning from the gate lodge, he made no reference to his adventure and when she tried to discuss the explosion with him, he changed the subject.

American sailors on the New York steamer *Honolulu* witnessed the explosion, the subsequent firing and incidents. They said that all the hotel windows were shattered. 'There was a wild stampede of dockers passing to work; they ran for safety to the Railway Stores nearby; two of them were hit by bullets, and, to add to the commotion, the women-folk of men working in the area all ran to the place.'

Several men in Martin's tried to draw Matt out on the morning's happenings, but he kept quiet about his arrest, though a few had seen him being placed against a wall and searched. By this time the struggle for freedom was at its height and the round of reprisals and counter-reprisals ended with the truce called in June and the talk of an Anglo Irish Treaty. Though the events of the five years from 1916 to 1921 must have stirred him as an Irishman and touched his life as a citizen of Dublin, they made little or no impact on his inner life. That life, silent, intense and hidden, continued to expand and grow; it surged strongly into every phase of his natural life, Matt Talbot's human existence flowing into and mingling with his interior life as the river with the sea.

Wages had risen in Martin's as in other firms since the 1913 strike, tradesmen receiving proportionately more than men without skills. Matt was still an unskilled labourer. He lacked the training that equipped others to do the kind of work that affords some pleasure, e.g. a carpentry job well finished. The satisfaction of achievement that repays, wholly or in part, the trouble involved in bringing the work to completion was not for Matt. Hundreds of men could have done his humble tasks, the only qualifications required being physical strength, endurance and the will to work. As has been seen, he had another occupation, a hidden one in which, apprenticed to Christ the Master Craftsman, he had acquired skill and found lasting joy. The rise in wages, though not a lot, was welcomed by him as a means of extending his charity. Martin's men, men in his sodality, neighbours in Rutland Street were not the only ones he helped. Every local and diocesan appeal found him ready to respond.

Martin's foreman in Castle Forbes was Mr Carew. He recalled how a Father Duffy from Tullyanna, Monaghan, called and asked permission to take up a collection from the workmen. Mr Carew told him to put up a notice saying that he could call on pay-day to take donations from the men for the charity he represented. On the Friday, when the men were paid, the priest returned and made his collection. Mr Carew takes up the story:

> When he was leaving I asked him if he had been up with Matt Talbot in Castle Forbes, knowing that Matt would be a certain subscriber. He had not known

about that part of the yard and went up. Later he came back to me and said 'I scruple about taking what the man up there gave me.' I asked him how much Matt had given him. 'All he had in his pay-packet', said the priest. Matt's pay-packet that day contained £3 ls 6d.

He left generous offerings in Gardiner Street church to buy flowers for the altars; once a week he sought out an old woman, 'gone in the head', who used sit in doorways smoking a pipe, and press money into her hand. From 1920 on he seems to have concentrated most of his almsgiving on the Foreign Missions, particularly the Maynooth Mission to China and the Holy Ghost missions in Nigeria. The Civil War began in 1922 when friend fought friend while brother killed brother. Cathal Brugha died fighting in July. Arthur Griffith, who never fired a shot, died in August of a heart attack. In August, too, those fellow fighters and old friends, Harry Boland and Michael Collins, now ranged on different sides, were killed.

Though his fellow workers sometimes poked fun at him, calling him Holy Joe or Old Diehard – this last because he admired Mr De Valera – they respected him. Those who knew him best said, 'We loved him.' A foreman recalled that whenever the weather was bad and he saluted Matt with 'That's a bad day', he got the reply, 'Every day that God sends is a good day', an attitude he retained even when his health deteriorated.

Fighting Ill Health

During 1923, Matt spent two periods in the Mater hospital, from 19 June to 17 July and from 10 September to 17 October. Professor Henry Moore was Senior Physician at the Mater and Professor of Medicine at University College Dublin. He was one of several witnesses who came forward to testify at the tribunals set up after Matt's death to enquire into his life. The doctor first came to know Matt when the latter came to see him before being admitted as a patient to the hospital in June 1923. Having diagnosed that Matt Talbot was suffering from a kidney and heart condition, he advised him to come into hospital for treatment. With great reluctance Matt allowed himself to be persuaded into doing so. The doctor stated:

> I got the impression that he was quite indifferent to his ailment and was prepared to accept whatever it pleased God to send him. While in hospital he behaved wonderfully as a patient and in a saintly manner. It occurred to me first that he might be a religious crank. I gathered that he gave away a good

deal of his money to others, and I had the impression that he left himself short of food.

Continuing his evidence Dr Moore said that the disease from which his patient suffered, while not painful in the ordinary sense, would give rise to considerable discomfort. In Matt's case it would have caused shortness of breath if he hurried or climbed stairs, and difficulty in breathing would make it hard for him to sleep.

The ward sister, Sister M. Veronica Frost, was in charge of St Laurence's Ward when Matt was admitted. The Sister remembered that he lay with his face to the wall when in the corridor; she had the impression that he was praying and took no interest in what went on around him. When able to walk a little, he said his Rosary as he walked, but hid the beads from the sight of others. Heart patients had to ask permission to use the lift when going up to the chapel, and Matt asked permission often; he was forbidden to kneel so he sat silent and motionless on the back seat.

On 27 October 1923, Matt was discharged from hospital. His friend, Ralph O'Callaghan, not having had a visit from Matt for almost six months, made enquiries about him, and went to the Mater to visit him in St

Laurence's Ward that autumn. When asked how he was, Matt said, 'Oh, I suffered, I suffered.' When he returned to 18 Rutland Street Mr O'Callaghan visited him again, bringing a £3 grant from the St Vincent de Paul Society of which he was a member. Some Vincent de Paul Brothers' leaflets in his books suggest that the society helped him at this period when he was very badly off.

His illness and frequent lack of money began to take their toll on him. When he paid the rent for his room he had sixpence a week left to live on. That would possibly have allowed him to live, having long since pared his needs to a minimum, but he could not continue his almsgiving. Fortunately Ralph O'Callaghan, the Vincent de Paul Brothers, the Lairds, Ned Fuller, the Larkins and other friends came from time to time; they would chat and, when leaving, would insist that Matt accept 'a little loan to tide you over, until you are back to form'.

Soon after Easter 1925 Mrs Manning, who had visited Matt while he was in hospital, was surprised to see him arrive in Martin's yard; he explained that he had come to see Mr Kelly, one of the principals of the firm, to get his job back or to get a small pension. Paddy Laird, however, remembers this quite differently, explaining that, knowing that Matt could be trusted to speak his mind and hoping to avoid another strike, the workmen urged Matt to ask Mr Kelly for an increase in wages, which had already been afforded to all workers but Matt and one other. Paddy Laird waited in Matt's hut to hear what happened.

I asked him how he got on. He said he asked why he hadn't been give the rise the other men got but Mr Kelly said, 'Surely you don't call yourself a workman?' 'Then I asked for a little pension, enough to help me to pay the rent of the room, and he said that T. & C. Martin's could not afford to pay pensions to all they employed.' And with that Matt sat down and began to cry. When he got control of himself I asked him was there anything more said. Matt replied, 'He said to me, "You don't smoke and you don't drink; though we cannot give you a pension we can give you back the job you had before you got sick".' So he cheered up but it struck me since that Matt was more ill than anyone thought. He came back the next day and everyone welcomed him. When he got his first week's wages he got Masses offered in thanksgiving for being taken back.

The day after his talk with Mr Kelly, Matt turned up for work at ten minutes to eight, punctual as ever. He did not know that after he left the previous day, the men who worked in his section went in a body to Mr Kelly's office and made it clear that they wanted Matt Talbot kept on in his job for the rest of his days; and, if he had to retire, they expected he would be given a pension in view of his long service and record as a worker. Mr Carew, the foreman, gave Matt a warm welcome. He thought him 'tired and wishy-washy looking', and warned him to take things easy. He also told men working in Matt's area to lend him a hand whenever they could do so quietly and not to let him carry too many planks. For the timber was heavy. Deals from Canada, ten or twelve feet long, two inches thick and nine inches wide. Matt always kept a pad on his shoulders, partly because the tar from the creosoted deals might drip on his clothes and partly because of his sloping shoulders – without the pad the planks would have slipped off.

From the day he returned to Martin's until his death Matt Talbot was never absent from work. More than forty years stood between the Matt of 1884 and the ageing man, now in his seventieth year, of 1925. During those years he had passed for a labouring man, dependable beyond the ordinary, careful and conscientious but silent and self-effacing. A privileged few knew him to be a man of constant prayer and bodily self-denial; fewer still knew of his nightly vigils, his brief repose on plank bed and wooden pillow. Only his confessor and director knew of God's dealings with the little working-man and of that interior life, hidden with Christ in God. To a friend who remarked on Matt's unremitting perseverance, he said, 'It's constancy God wants.'

Victory in Death

The heatwave that had parched Europe and America in May 1925 reached Dublin a little later. Whit Sunday (31 May), and the bank holiday (1 June), were exceptionally cold, with showers of hail and rain; but by mid-week the city sweltered under a broiling sun. The barometer soared and Trinity Sunday, 7 June, dawned in a haze of heat. The hospitals were kept busy and ambulances were in constant demand.

On that Sunday, which he always kept as a special feast, Matt Talbot was out early intent on completing his programme of prayers and Masses. The previous month he had entered his seventieth year. Age was beginning to tell on him. In former days he would be at Masses in different churches from early morning, fasting all the time, and ending with one o'clock Mass at the Pro-Cathedral, mother-church of the Archdiocese, St Mary's of the Immaculate Conception, where he had been baptised.

There is no reason to suppose that he received any fore-warning that the Trinity Sunday of 1925 was to be a day of days for him. Even if he had had a premonition he would not have made any change in the Sunday routine he had followed since his illness. To him it was not routine, but the re-enactment and renewal of Calvary as Mass succeeded Mass. For him his union with Christ in the eucharistic sacrifice and sacrament was a fountainhead of unfailing joy and peace.

Though the morning was very warm, Matt hurried so as to be in time for the ten o'clock Mass in St Saviour's, the Dominican church. As he turned into the laneway, a short-cut to the church, he ran a few steps, stumbled and collapsed. A visitor from Rugby, a Mr O'Brien, was coming behind Matt:

> He was walking less than five feet in front of me, I saw him shudder, partly turn and fall to the ground. I ran to him as also did a young man named Walsh. We loosened his shirt-collar but I knew he was dead. I ran to Dominick Street Priory and brought a priest. When the priest saw him he knew that life had left him. We knelt down and prayed for the repose of his soul.

Others emerging from the nine o'clock Mass or coming for the next Mass joined O'Brien and Walsh and carried Matt from where he fell at the right-hand side. Two boys, more knowing than their friends, ran to Parnell Square to fetch Garda O'Hanlon who was on duty there. Dr Eustace came, examined the unknown man and pronounced him dead. Once the ambulance arrived his body was removed to the mortuary in Jervis Street Hospital. When Charles Manners, a mortuary attendant, and the porter undressed the corpse they found a cord on one arm, a small chain on the other:

> I was cutting his clothing with a scissors when I found a larger chain, with links about half-an-inch long, the size of a horse's trace, wound round the body. There was also a chain below the knee, so placed that it must have caused him great mortification when kneeling; he had a cord below the other knee. We sent for Sister Ignatius and showed her the chains.

The witnesses' evidence, given several years later, is somewhat confusing. One described the chains as rusted, another as bright. One thought they had been worn for years; the porter said they were not embedded in the flesh, but that they had worn grooves in the skin which was slightly reddened. More sensation was caused by the discovery of Matt's chains than by any aspect of his life.

According to John Gunning, when he and Matt were enrolled at Clonliffe College, they had 'little iron chains, like the chains in a clock'. They were not the only people in Ireland enrolled in the True Devotion during the 1920s and 1930s. The late Frank Duff, founder of the Legion of Mary, recommended it strongly to the Legionaries. Moreover, missionary orders preparing novices for the rigours of life in primitive mission fields, also encouraged the wearing of the small chain. However, the terms slave and slavery were off-putting to many Irish people, just then beginning to savour freedom from the bondage of foreign rule.

During the first five months of 1925 Matt Talbot was a sick old man, but an old man intent on doing more and more for God; the only way he could think of doing this was by wearing bigger and heavier chains.

The men in Martin's yards were astounded when they heard of the chains found on his dead body; they declared that he could not possibly have done the heavy work he did while wearing chains, 'and Matt would do as much in one hour as others in two', one said, 'besides, some of us would have noticed it sometime'. This, combined with the Mater evidence for 1923, suggests that he did not wear them constantly. His devotion to Our Lady would have prompted him to wear them on Saturdays, her special day; while Sunday, the Lord's Day, was a day when he always practised extra penance. The last word on the chains must be left to his friends and neighbours: 'Matt would have been forgotten the day he died only for the chains: and God gave him the kind of death he got to show the world the sort of man Matt Talbot was.'

Although he died on Sunday 7 June, Matt Talbot was not buried until the following Thursday, the feast of Corpus Christi. On the Wednesday Ralph O'Callaghan learned, quite by accident, of his friend's death and at once took responsibility for the funeral expenses. He also sent word to Father Flood in the Pro-Cathedral, who had previously been in St Laurence O'Toole's and who knew Matt to see and by reputation. John Robins, Ted Fuller and Paddy Laird helped to carry the coffin into Gardiner Street church. Few were present when the coffin was placed in the Sacred Heart chapel; there, on the vigil of the feast of the Blessed Sacrament, the dead man lay where the living man had so often worshipped.

Thursday 11 June was a Church holiday and Matt's funeral took place after eleven o'clock Mass. Besides the Fylan and Andrews families and some neighbours from

Rutland Street there were men from T. & C. Martin's and members of Matt's sodality. Father Flood and Mr O'Callaghan were also present. Dublin being a most sociable city there were many spectators. Already people were speaking of Matt Talbot; his austerities, so long a secret shared with God alone, were no longer unknown. For over forty years he had hidden what he called his 'way of life'. The suddenness of his end revealed what he would have concealed had he got warning of death's approach.

The funeral was a very ordinary one: an elm coffin, a hearse and four white-plumed horses, a mourning coach and two carriages. The cost, including the removal of the remains from Jervis Street Hospital, was £10. The grave was No. SK 319½ in St Bridget's section of the cemetery. Six years later Father Murphy and the men of Matt's sodality in Gardiner Street purchased the adjoining grave space, SK 320, and asked the Cemeteries Committee not to allow any further burial in the two-grave plot. Permission was granted and the sodality given control of the plot.

Matt Talbot's life story became so well known that in 1931 an inquiry was inaugurated by the then Archbishop, Dr Byrne. Its first session was held on the feast of All the Saints of Ireland, 6 November. This was the first step of the strict procedure followed before any holy person is beatified and allowed to be honoured in any one diocese, country or religious order. If, eventually, the beatus is canonised, the veneration is extended to the entire Church. When the Informative, or diocesan enquiry, ended a carefully collated and authenticated copy of the witnesses' sworn evidence was forwarded to the Holy See. Similarly, at the end of the Apostolic Process or inquiry in 1953, when a greater number of witnesses was interrogated, the evidence was sent to Rome. A papal decree introducing Matt's Cause was signed in 1937.

Canon law regulations for Causes requires that such evidence must be presented in longhand. A team of Dominican nuns was given the task of transcribing the accumulated evidence. The traditional illuminative style of ancient Irish manuscripts was supplied by an artistically gifted Dominican Sister. She must have been drained of energy when she completed the fourteen hundred pages which were then bound in four volumes and sent on to Rome.

In 1952 Matt Talbot's remains were exhumed and removed to a vault in the central circle of the cemetery, near the tomb of Hogan the sculptor. Distinguished ecclesiastics and lay people were present, including the

President of Ireland, Sean T. Ó'Ceallaigh who, as an altar-boy, had known Matt and had often seen him praying in Berkeley Road church. When the remains were identified they were transferred to a double coffin, the outer oaken coffin having a brass plate affixed with the inscription:

THE SERVANT OF GOD
MATTHEW TALBOT

The same inscription was on a marble plaque placed over the iron gate of the vault, the coffin being visible through the railing of the gate. To that grave, from 1952 to 1972, pilgrims from far and near came to pray. The unemployed of the city trudged to Glasnevin asking Matt to find them work. Missionaries leaving for distant mission fields came to ask the man who so generously helped their work in his lifetime to continue to aid them. Returned exiles and foreign tourists also found their way to Matt's grave.

Standing and praying there one day among the gathering was an illustrious pilgrim, the future Pope Paul VI who would go on to declare Matt venerable in 1975. Then Cardinal Montini, he was staying with President de Valera at Áras an Uachtaráin; preferring to remain incognito, he cycled from the Park to Glasnevin and, dressed as a priest, paid his respects to one whose life story he had read and in whose Cause he was deeply interested.

No other tomb in that place of noble monuments attracted so many visitors. More than one poet found inspiration there, among them Liam Brophy who penned these lines:

> Although no pomp attend him,
> The stream's procession all day long
> Files past him, and the stately throng
> Of surpliced clouds, from rim to rim
> Of heaven, pass him, and the song
> Of seabirds, where dim islands loom,
> Makes requiem above his tomb.
>
> And though no canopy was spread
> Above his wrinkled corpse, each night
> A swift angelic acolyte
> Enkindles stars above his head;
> And reverentially and light
> The cool asperges of the rain
> Fall on that form, once hot with pain.

Epilogue

Twenty years later, in 1972, the remains were again removed, this time to a church in the heart of the city, Our Lady of Lourdes in Sean MacDermott Street, in the area where Matt spent his life. The tomb of Wicklow granite has a glass panel in front, through which the coffin may be seen. Day in, day out, people come to pray at that tomb, some in ones and twos, others in organised pilgrimages hundreds strong, from overseas as well as from all parts of Ireland. They pray to Matt, asking him to intercede for them; and they pray for him, that he may soon be raised to the altars of the Church and given the titles of Blessed and Saint.

Saints are saints, however, not because of the official proclamation, but because they are holy. God, not the proclamation, makes the saint. The secret of Matt's attraction is his holiness, for sanctity has a magnetism all its own. It is indeed something to ponder and wonder at, that a poor man, almost unknown in life, should become famous in death and acquire an influence which extends far beyond the boundaries of Dublin, indeed beyond the shores of his native land. On the building sites a century ago, foremen put Matt first on the line of hod-men 'to set the pace'. It has pleased God, the Master-Builder, in the building of that city not made with hands, to raise up Matt Talbot – *pauper, servus et humilis*, poor, serving and lowly – and put him before us, to set the pace.

Prayers

Prayer for the Canonisation of Matt Talbot

Lord, in your servant, Matt Talbot you
have given us a wonderful example of
triumph over addiction, of devotion to
duty, and of lifelong reverence for the
Holy Sacrament. May his life of
prayer and penance give us courage
to take up our crosses and follow in the
footsteps of Our Lord and Saviour,
Jesus Christ.

Father, if it be your will that your
beloved servant should be glorified by
your Church, make known by your
heavenly favours the power he enjoys in
your sight. We ask this through the
same Jesus Christ Our Lord. Amen.

Matt Talbot

Asking Matt's Help in the Presence of the Lord

Gentle Matt, I turn to you in my present needs and ask for the help of your prayers.

Trusting in you, I am confident your charitable and understanding heart will make my petitions your own.

I believe that you are truly powerful in the presence of Divine Mercy. If it be for the glory of the Sacred Heart of Jesus, the honour of Mary, our Mother and Queen and the deepening of my relationship with them, show that your goodness towards me, in my daily struggles, equals your influence with the Holy Spirit, who is hidden and at home in my Heart.

Friend of pity, friend of power, hear, oh hear me in this hour, gentle Matt, please pray for me.